TH INGS

Y

I LIED

THIS IS

Y

I LIED

ANDREW J. ANDERSON

GET WRITE PUBLISHING

This is Y I Lied

Copyright © 2020 by Andrew J. Anderson

ISBN: 978-1-7342508-9-3

Cover Design:
Rekesha Pittman and US Entarprise

Editor: Get Write LLC

Get Write Publishing
14850 Montfort Drive – Suite 290
Dallas, TX 75254

Printed in the United States of America.

DEDICATION

To everyone affected by the false image of me: My family, my church family, and my youth group.

FOREWORD

Andrew and I became friends through the arts. I served as Stage Manager for his stage production, "This House Was Built for Tough Times." I had no idea how difficult those times really were.

When I hosted dance concerts, Drew would serve as my emcee. He always had a way of getting the audience to respond to him with so much enthusiasm. His personality was beaming.

One year, I suspected that something different was happening with Andrew. I couldn't quite put my finger on it. I called him on the phone and asked, "Is your life right with God?" He said yes. "Are you sure?" I asked. "Yes!" he replied. He hosted the church event one last time. After that, we drifted apart.

Social media gave us a window into each other's lives. I saw a video that he posted where he spoke at a church about wearing a mask. That is how I found out the truth about my friend.

I didn't gasp. I didn't call anyone. I wasn't disappointed. Drew was Drew.

He would message me and I would message him. When He didn't respond, I never took it personally. I believe that life has a way of perfect timing and that true friendship is always renewable.

When we initially spoke about releasing his story, things took off quickly, then came to a halt. I wasn't sure that we would ever release this work. Suddenly, he contacted me and let me know that it was time to release the book. It is my honor to help him and many others heal in this way.

Andrew J. Anderson is one of the realest people I know. I am honored to call him a friend and to serve as the midwife for his story. What's your "Y?" Be open as Andrew reveals his.

Rekesha Pittman

Get Write Publishing

TABLE OF CONTENTS

Dear Journal ...

With a made-up mind, thoughts of my life will be written down in this black journal of mine. These are the things I'll never share with anyone. If anyone ever wanted to know about me and finds this journal, here is where I will be exposed. This is where all my secrets are. I trust you, journal. I know you will never tell.

-Drew

This is the Andrew
you thought you once knew...

This was the journal that turned out to be my book, my story, and my life. You will have an encounter with the many masks of me. This is the Andrew that finally confronted the past and is now living to tell you about it. I will share my pains, various struggles, misguided feelings, lies, betrayal, deceit and trickery. This was once my life.

To reveal this now isn't easy. I was afraid of releasing this truth. The biggest obstacle is the fear of what you will say once your eyes have scoured this book.

I knew it had to be done. I can no longer walk around with these memories inside my head. I couldn't walk in my truth while living in fear and bondage for your approval any longer.

If lying was a drug, I was definitely addicted and hooked. I didn't know how to stop lying. I lied for so long that it became a part of me. This is my story.

I never had intentions of letting this out—EVER! Revisiting my past has brought me much pain, but it has also given me much understanding. I'm no longer ashamed. I am who I am.

I now realize that my writings aren't just for me, but for someone reading this. It's for the young man who believes God has given up on him because he is gay. It's for the preacher who is married but can't tell his wife the truth. It's for the reader who believes that being gay is a sin. It may be for a girl who is in love with another girl but is afraid to let anyone else know.

Because you have read this far means a lot. I thank you. I'm inviting you into my life. Leave your judgment, opinions, concerns, and religious beliefs at the door.

I'm not here to debate with you about what you believe to be true concerning me. Take off your shoes and come into my heart. Cry with me. You may even laugh at or with me. You may very well change with me.

I acknowledge that some of you reading this will be hurt, but I hope that you will hear me out. I have hurt a lot of people and betrayed many. It is now my responsibility to make amends.

I hid and lied because I was afraid. I feared what you all would say about me. I wanted to please each and every one of you. I wanted you all to be happy with me.

I didn't write this book to make an announcement as though I am proud and boastful. I wrote it to tell each and every one "Y." Let me define my "Y." I had questions that only I could give honest responses to. I finally came to a place where I could explain my whys. That's the reason for this book.

We all have a life to live—whether in the public or private sector of our lives. We all have our truths to bear. We each have journeys and paths. I wanted to walk free, but I had the chains of my past attached to me.

I have picked up this story so many times and put it back down so many times because I wanted each part to be as truthful as I am. It had to happen as my journey unfolded. I had to write according to what I felt I needed to say. I didn't want to leave anything out.

I have taken the pieces of my life and placed them within these pages. I went through my journals to figure out what I believed was important. Some of these are my personal journal entries.

I'm not telling on anyone. I'm not calling anyone out. I'm not telling you someone else's story.

I was hurting. I had pains that Tylenol couldn't stop. Advil couldn't relieve me. Vicodin could only put me to sleep. Alcohol only had a temporary effect. I had pains that doctors couldn't diagnose and x-rays couldn't find. I had hurts that only truth could heal.

My masks are being stripped away and I choose not to wear them ever again. I was just going to live my life in a way that allowed me to remain silent. I struggled silently. I cried privately. I wore a mask daily! I was going to continue to assign myself different roles to play throughout my life to keep me out of people's mouths.

I couldn't tell folks that the guy they knew as Andrew then wasn't real. He was born a homosexual. He hid it.

What about the girls I dated or the woman I married? What about all of the sermons I preached? What about the youth I taught at Bible study while I was entrusted with their lives?

Remember songs I led in the choir? The testimonies I gave? The young boy became a man of God filled with the burning Holy Ghost. Oh, noooooo... not me! I wasn't going out like that.

I had an entire scenario planned out in my head. *What are they going to say? What are they going to think? How will I ever be able to show my face to my friends and family? Should I just leave the church scene? Should I move away? What if I change my phone number so that only my immediate family could contact me?* I was going crazy.

WARNING

Before you go any further—and I mean it—I suggest that you close this book and never open it again if you cannot handle my truth. I use expressive language and some of the material in here is explicit. I'm not holding back.

I can already hear some of you saying, "Why did Andrew put all of his business out there like that?" "He could've just kept that to himself." "Everybody didn't have to know!" "I thought we were close. You should've come to me first before I read the book." "Why did you wait until now to say something?"

These same questions made me put down my pen and keep hiding. I knew that the only way out was to use my experiences, gather my writings, and press print.

Now that I have come to my truth, I realize that it was never homosexuality that I was struggling with; it was how I would be viewed after I told someone. I couldn't share this story with my Baptist upbringing.

There were others who had never been to church and were enjoying the lives given to them. I was ready to be delivered—not from the lifestyle of homosexuality—from **people**. I had to get to a place where I didn't care what people said or how they looked at me. I had to be secure and lovingly accept me for me. Now, when folks email me or say things like, "I'm praying for your deliverance," I kindly reassure them: "I'm already delivered!"

I will not mention any names, except for those I have permission to use. So, don't go skipping pages to see what I did with whom because it's not in here. Yes, I'm looking at *you*. I will only tell on myself. So, come on this journey with me.

DREW'S JOURNAL

May 7, 2001

Who actually knows my true thoughts, my true intentions, my true motives, or my real desires? What about my silent struggles, my frustrations, my fears, my strengths, or my weaknesses? I sit back and ask myself those questions.

So many thoughts flutter across my mind right now that I don't know what to do or where to begin to figure it out. How can I examine myself when I'm afraid to really see me? I mean, everything should be going well in my life right now. I'm a preacher, called and chosen by the highest God, soon-to-be husband, and friend to a beautiful woman.

Sometimes I don't feel like a preacher; sometimes I can't stand being a preacher. Do I really love God or do I love Him when it's convenient for me?

why do I keep falling into the same sinful trap the Lord is leading me out of?

I teach the youth. I lay hands on the children. I prophesy to people and I'm still scared because I don't want to hear You say "Depart from Me."

I just want that same anointing You instilled in me a long time ago. I miss the chills and the way You moved when Your Spirit was so strong upon me. I want to be back in Your presence where I once dwelled.

Lead me, God. Deliver me from my mind and my emotions. I'm so sleepy, God. I'm a messed-up individual. I am heartless, cruel, and a liar.

Chapter 1

THIS IS

Y

I GOT MARRIED

Where do I begin? I have so much to say. I'm now at a place in my life where I'm able to tell all and not be ashamed.

There was a period in my life when I felt that as long as people didn't know about me, I was fine skating by and living many different lives. At times, I thought I was bi-polar and people were actually calling me that. I started to believe it. I laugh now.

I felt like I needed to see a therapist and required meds—something to help me diagnose my problem. I was driving myself crazy. I was chasing myself. I wanted my life to finally catch up to the one I thought was planned out for me.

My life became a script for a gospel play. You know, the kind of plays where everything comes together in the end: The family goes back to being happy, the homosexual turns heterosexual and dates women... that stuff. Well, that wasn't in my script.

For so long, I got tired of acting in everyone else's story. I played different characters while denying myself. I was doing my best to please everyone. So, what were some of the roles I sought out to fill? I auditioned and got the part of the HUSBAND!

The morning of the wedding, I woke up looking at myself in the bathroom mirror. I asked myself the question, "How did you manage to get this far into this?" I was afraid to back out because the lease on the apartment was already signed, the reception was paid for in full, and my fiancée was getting beautiful for a church full of family and friends.

Snap out of it, Drew! It's too late! You already accepted the part/role when you proposed. You can do this! You make a beautiful couple and she will be the perfect preacher's wife. After all, she is beautiful and she's a worshipper. She has a sincere relationship with God. This is the one for you.

I literally felt like Macaulay Culkin in "Home Alone" when he looked into the mirror and said, "This is it, don't get scared now."

What do I do? I couldn't admit to any-one that I was scared as hell because I didn't know what I was doing. I stood at the altar, numb. In front of me were hundreds of people. I was about to get **MARRIED**!

Everything seemed to go by so fast that day. I watched as the Pastor's lips moved, but I couldn't feel my legs. I just had to be prepared to say, "**I do.**"

I was nervous the entire time. I looked like I had it all together, but I didn't. I didn't want to be a homosexual, so I played the role of a heterosexual in hopes that being married would be the ultimate cure of my homosexuality.

Our wedding ceremony and vows went smoothly. It was almost too perfect. Next was the reception.

Most heterosexual men would probably want to rush through the entire reception for the sexual lovemaking that is expected at the end of the night. I, on the other hand, wanted the reception to last all night long. I was thinking things like, *I hope she is tired and goes to sleep after she gets out of her dress because I'm tired. What if I don't get hard?* Before I knew it, we were in bed and I was the "husband."

I now had to assume responsibility for someone other than me. It really didn't hit me until the next morning when we didn't have transportation to get from the hotel back to our apartment. We didn't drive our cars to the hotel, so I had to think about how to provide a way home for us.

Our marriage was exciting for the first couple of months before reality set in. I wasn't making sexual advances. It was like we had become roommates.

One night during a mild conversation she asked, "Are you gay? You probably are and just can't be honest enough to say anything!" It was like she had an intuition about me or maybe she was just upset. At that point, I fought with everything within to keep from crying.

Her question stung because she was right. I denied it with a straight face. It hurt because something was clearly telling her that she married an actor. Her hurt and anger made me see that I was still gay. I thought that over time I would become the heterosexual I thought I was born to be.

I was actually mad and couldn't do anything about it. I didn't know how to respond; I just knew I had to respond in a defensive manner. I wasn't going to tell her the truth. At that time, I knew that our marriage was already hitting rock bottom. We separated, which ultimately led to our divorce.

She had a valid reason for divorcing me: I lied about everything. I lied about my credit, which we discussed prior to becoming a team. I lied about helping to pay for the wedding, when the truth was, I was already struggling financially. I lied about my car being towed and said that I parked it in the red at work, when actually it got repossessed. I lied about the money that was being taken from my account for taxes that I hadn't paid. I lied about some of the bills being paid when they weren't.

I lied when I took my vows. I was lying when I asked her out on a date. My entire marriage was a lie and I was trying to make it my truth.

If I lied about the bills, I would lie about everything else. I took her through that whirlwind only to see if I could be a heterosexual. I involved her family and my family in my world of lies. I wish I could take it all back.

While married, I had thoughts and fantasies of being with other men. I never slept with a man while I was married. It would get so bad that I even began going to the video store and picking out gay porn to watch when she was away. I would watch videos before she came home. I even lied to the guy that worked at the video store about why and who I was getting the porn for.

I had built my entire marriage on a lie. Our engagement and dating period were built on a lie. I did it all because that's what I thought I could get away with.

She never deserved any of that. She trusted me with her life but I didn't trust myself. Part of me thought it would all disappear.

I wish I could rewind to the day I walked into her life. I would have merely been her friend, but don't even think I could have been that either.

I lied because what she had felt in her heart was right. I lied because I wanted it to be perfect for all who had wanted it. I wanted the wedding and to know what it felt like to be standing at the altar looking at a beautiful woman in white walking towards me. I wasn't prepared for what was coming after we said, "I do." I just had hopes that it would all go away one day while being married. I knew that I wanted to be her husband because if I didn't marry her, people would begin to talk.

DREW'S JOURNAL

August 23, 2002

What do you do when your heart can't choose which beat it wants to follow? What do you do when your heart misses a beat and can't figure out when the next one is coming? My heart is beating faster than a bullet because it's falling to pieces, minute by minute.

Wait... I heard another harsh word that shot me to my heart. Will I die this time? I can't cry. The bleeding words inside have captured my soul and they won't let go because of this thing called pride.

Stop. Stop! My heart can't take any more. Just go ahead and go. Walk your tired ass out the door. Better yet, you stay since your name is on the lease anyway.

I'll pack up my things, toss the wedding ring and pray to God for some better things. Wait... what was that you just said? You've got another man who's going to love you for you?

Damn. I thought that was what I was trying to do. I'm going to be alright. I'll make it just fine. I'm just glad my heart is still beating—this time.

Chapter 2

THIS IS

Y

I STARTED
DRINKING

Bittersweet emotions filled my world as I faced moving back in with my mom. It was a world I wasn't ready to face because a divorce comes with questions. I wanted to avoid hearing "I told you so" and the embarrassment of dealing with a failed marriage.

How was I going to explain what happened without sharing too much info? I was trying to have my answers prepared for questions that hadn't been asked yet. I couldn't blame it on anyone because there was no one else to blame. I came to the realization that you cannot blame the truth.

Going through my divorce was a very bitter and draining time. I was fighting false emotions. Internally, I was upset because it didn't work. I felt like I had let a lot of people down. I lost a battle that I just knew I was going to win.

There I was, trying to suppress all of me for the way others perceived me. It was *their* fairytale ending for their prince charming, Andrew. Not mine.

It was all too much for me to deal with, so I started drinking cheap wine. Once I conquered wine, I moved on to hard liquor. I drank to avoid dealing with what was really happening to me.

One night while staying with my mom, I drank so much that I ended up on my mom's floor, blanketed by my own vomit. Once I was able to get up, I made my way to the bathroom to take a bath but ended up vomiting into the water.

My chest started hurting. Each regurgitation felt like someone was punching me. There I was, laughing while drunk. I had clearly lost my mind. At the time, I wasn't concerned with who saw me or who was going to know. The truth was, I didn't know how to deal with my reality.

I remember celebrating my 25th birthday. People were buying drinks for me. I was a newbie at drinking, so I didn't know anything about mixing dark liquor with clear liquor.

I was introduced to the Adios Mother Fucker (which bears truth to its name)— wine, Patron shots, and so much liquor on an empty stomach! I didn't drink any water nor did I eat, which made me regret ever drinking anything at all the next morning. I was so drunk that I didn't remember how I got home, how I got out of the car, or how I ended up in my bed.

When I woke up the next morning, it was like experiencing millions of tractors running inside my head at the same time. I was in so much pain that it hurt to open my eyes. It was even worse to drink water, let alone hear the name of alcohol.

I threw up as soon as I thought about alcohol. It wasn't a pretty sight. I couldn't eat anything. That was my very first hangover.

It's amazing how much my mind goes back to retrieve the memories embedded in my head. I promised myself that I would never tell a soul. I was in pain physically and emotionally. I would still go to church and smile while crying on the inside.

I was upset with the rumors that were being spread while my divorce was being finalized. I would hear people talk. I said nothing. I just acted as if I had it all together; yet another role I was playing to present a false security.

I would still show my face each and every Sunday because I wanted to make it known that I was going to be alright. I was still praising and leading songs while touching the lives of everyone else but my own. I was role-playing. At the time, it was easier being someone else other than me.

Chapter 3

THIS IS

Y

I TRIED

TO PRAY

THE GAY AWAY

While back home with Mama, I was determined to live right. I just knew I didn't like the person I had become, so I went on a 15-day fast to "Pray the gay away." There was no masturbation, no porn, no sex talk, or no sex with anyone. I had to be in the bed by 9:00 p.m. and wake up at 6:00 a.m. for prayer and meditation.

I made up in my mind that I would shut my phone off at a certain hour. It was yet another trick to try and cure my homosexuality. This one had to work because the Bible said that a type of power comes with fasting and prayer. I was fasting for a renewed mind. I was sure that I was going to beat the gay "spirit" away. After all, it was just a "spirit" and "spirits" could be driven out, right?

I wasn't going to feed into it. I was going to starve my flesh. I wasn't going to watch television, listen to music, or even look at men. It was the spiritual way to become a heterosexual.

Others began thinking I was on a deep inner cleansing for healing and restoration. The truth was, I was fasting *not* to be gay! *Get it out of me! Remove it! I don't want it! I don't like it! Just get it far away from me as possible.* I was crying out to God, "Where did it come from?" "Why is it here?" "Why **me**?"

The more I tried to contain myself, the more I wanted to rebel. My hormones were raging. I couldn't walk around without having an erection. I was putting myself through punishment. Why was I torturing myself like this?

One night I grabbed a porn tape, pulled out my penis, and tried not to break it while masturbating so hard. I broke that fast after just one week. I tried marriage and that didn't make me a heterosexual, so why in the hell was I fooling myself with this shit?

One day I was reading a newspaper and landed in the personal ads. What struck my interest was the section labeled "Men for Men." I was nervous because I was trying to figure out how to pull that off while still living with my mama.

I had a nervous energy throughout my body. I wanted to call, but I didn't want it to show up on the phone bill. So, I ended up getting my own phone line in my room so that I could have some privacy. I mean, how harmful could it be? No one sees my face, right?

I listened to personal ads placed by other men. As I would listen, I would get excited because those men were looking for the same thing I was.

I got the courage to place my own ad it went like this (deepens voice): "Yo, this is D. I'm 5'9", 220 pounds, bald headed, goatee, masculine, living in Long Beach. You must drive and have your own place. I do not host. I'm aggressive and enjoy sex. If you are interested, leave me a message." I pressed the number one to finalize my message and it was out there for others to hear.

Not even 15 minutes passed and I had a full box of voice messages. They left their phone numbers, penis sizes, chest measurements, waist measurements, and even their shoe sizes. It was crazy, but it was actually fun.

I didn't know what I was getting myself into. I was enjoying the attention from men who had never seen me but liked what I put out there. I would call them and get to know who they were over the phone. Then, we would meet.

Meeting those men opened a world of sex, sex, and more sex! If the description sounded interesting enough, I would call. I met guys at coffee shops, parking lots, restaurants, public parks, and even at their homes. I wasn't thinking about my safety or what could happen to me. I just knew that line was for hookups.

Sometimes their phone description would not match their actual in-person appearance but I didn't have the guts to say no once I was in their presence. It was too late. By that point, I wasn't going to start the search over again.

In retrospect, I could've been robbed, jumped, stabbed or even killed meeting with people I didn't know. I trusted that they were just like me and that nothing harmful could happen. I was nice and respectable. I believed that since they were homosexuals, it wasn't a threat to my life.

I was sneaking in through backdoors, garages, and even in cars. I had sex with men that had kids in the next room or parents sleeping nearby. Sometimes, the instructions would be just to walk in because the door was unlocked.

I would walk into dark rooms and feel my way around for a toe or some type of body part. It didn't matter what time it was. My late-night rendezvous would be in the wee hours of the morning. I could wake up and check the line, then respond to a request. I was on a mission and on the prowl.

After a while, I knew the tricks of the party line. If I wanted the thugs, I had to be direct and speak that slang. I also had to mention that I had a girl. If I wanted conservative, husband-like men, I would use educated speech and be very discreet. If I sought the submissive type that did everything I wanted in the bedroom, I would just say, "Leave a message with what you want me to do to you."

I encountered so many different types of men on the party line. I had the choice to dabble in all types of men if I chose to—Caucasian, Latino, Chinese, African-American, Filipino, Indian, fat, skinny, athletic, blind, handicapped, married, divorced, newlywed, teachers, preachers, Sunday school teachers, professors, construction workers—everything you could imagine. I would often ask myself, "Drew, what in the hell are you doing? Are you there? Answer me, dammit!"

I was meeting men at hotels; some were on business trips while others liked the privacy of being away from their families. Eventually, I started driving in a neighborhood in Long Beach to see what I could get within the hour. Some nights would be good while other nights were a waste of my time.

Was I prostituting? In a way, I was; I just wasn't getting any money at the end. I was giving my body away for minutes of pure satisfaction. I was a true sex whore!

It didn't matter who it was. If we connected via phone, we would meet instantly. I would see a guy, talk for a few minutes, and then have sex. Once we were done, I left. I put my clothes back on and walked out. It meant nothing to me. I didn't want a relationship; I just wanted my sexual desires met.

DREW'S JOURNAL

March 4, 2004

I was on my way to sleep last night and the phone rang. I got up, got dressed and went to his house. The guy from yesterday needed to wash out his ass. Oh, my gosh! All I smelled was ass in the air. Stinky, sweaty ass! I couldn't even stay hard. Ugggghhh! I told him to go take a shower and I left!

Tonight, I just got in from yet another midnight scandal. It was actually good. He really knows what he is doing.

We were in all types of positions. I didn't even have to tell him what to do, he just did it. Make a nigga wanna come back for more.

My lips are swollen because he was biting the hell out of them and sucking them like candy. I'm not complaining!

Hopefully, we will meet up tomorrow night so he can get the fuck knocked out of him, AGAIN.

DREW'S JOURNAL

March 15, 2004

I must be some kind of new fool. I don't know what I got myself into. Here it goes...

Friday night, I met up with this new fling. He was not cute, but decent enough for the job that needed to be done. The downfall of the evening was that he smoked, but he can suck the hell out of some dick. That felt hella good.

It took me some time to bust a nut, but I came. He offered me some Hypnotic afterwards and then we talked. I didn't just get up and leave, which was odd. Now, I'm all screwed up.

Yesterday, I smoked a joint with my dad. I didn't get high or anything, but the fact that I did it scares me. What am I doing? I haven't prayed. I haven't spoken to the Lord in a while.

My whole disposition of church has changed. I don't look at people the same. I'm just to the point of enjoying what it is whatever it is I am doing.

There are just so many diseases out there. I guess I feel bad that I'm doing all these wrong and disobedient things to my soul and body. I can't go to God because I know I'm going to go right back and do it again.

If I'm not careful... Oh, shit! I have consequences that I have to deal with. This is so crazy.

DREW'S JOURNAL

March 19, 2004

I just got back from his house. It was good again tonight. His breath was tart... Oh, well. we were sexing.

It was really good. So far, he's the best. I was all up in him, deep. He said he wasn't ready, but his ass was telling me different.

I don't know how much longer I can keep doing this. It's bound to stop sometime. This is soooo wrong.

I believe I have a hickey on my neck because my neck is burning. He bit a good chunk of it. DAMN, I'm good! Out of the past few guys I've slept with, this one is by far the bomb!

DREW'S JOURNAL

April 2, 2004

OK! The shit I do for some ass. I'm back from his house again.

For some reason, he is really ugly to me. I actually got a good look at his face tonight. He really does have big teeth. I guess that's all the more reason why my dick hurts when I leave his house. His breath was tart again. Next time, I'm going to let him know.

I'm playing risky business. I almost did it without a condom. You never know what people have. I don't care how fine you are; you could be an S.T.D. waiting to happen.

Drew, no more playing it that close without protection. I just checked out my neck. DAMMIT, I have another hickey. Shit!

Chapter 4

THIS IS

Y

I STAYED IN THE CLOSET

The phone lines eventually led to me meeting men I already knew who didn't know I was a closeted homosexual. I didn't know that they were in the closet either.

It was getting really scary because I didn't want what I did to leak out. After all, I was Christian. I had a position in the church and was known within the church community. At the same time, they didn't want their cover blown either. As long as what we did stayed between us, it was a match.

I was the night stalker. Everything I did took place at night. I found many things to do and places to go at night.

I would leave my mom's house and arrive back by the time they would just be waking up. Although I had a car, I would have guys pick me up from my mom's house or down the street from my mom's house. I did that to play it safe because I didn't know the backgrounds of the men that would visit.

I had to keep it a complete secret from my family. I also didn't want my mom peeking her head outside to see who I was leaving with.

Not only did the phone lines lead to meeting men, it led me to a man who introduced me to the West Hollowood scene. We began dating. Actually, he was the first guy I truly dated. That relationship was fun.

He was very respectable and good looking. I didn't know how to act because it was my first closet relationship with a man. He made sure that I was taken care of in every way. I knew about the West Hollowood scene but had never walked the streets of it.

It was there that I was awakened to yet another world I wasn't ready for. The Rage was the club that exposed me to men dancing in Speedos with oily bodies. The Rage revealed that there was really a world of men who weren't ashamed of who they were.

I never knew that one night would lead to many more nights of taking trips alone. It became a weekly thing for me to do. I would leave church Sunday evenings and head to West Hollywood. The nights I would go alone would be the nights I often found myself having sex in my car or theirs. Crazy… Horny… STUPID! Whatever you wanted to call it; I was.

I never wanted to run into anyone I knew. I would go to clubs that were dark and would stay near the back so that I had the chance to see everyone who came in the door.

One night, I saw one of my cousin's friends and just knew my world was about to turn upside down. I froze. I tried to maneuver into a dark space without causing a scene. My first instinct was to run out the door, but what was that going to prove? We had seen each other already and I knew he was going to call my cousin, so I walked over to him and greeted him. I nicely told him not to tell anyone he saw me.

He didn't know it, but I was upset. I wasn't mad with him at all. I was more upset by the fact that I had been caught.

Guilt can cause the biggest attitudes. One minute, you could be smiling. Next, you'll be upset without knowing why. I didn't want anyone to know beyond the ones who already knew. The only reason some knew of my secret life was because I knew about theirs. I wanted *that* life to be separate.

I was living entirely way too many lives and couldn't keep up with myself. The West Hollywood life became boring to me, so I started going to Jewel's Catch One. It was a club in Los Angeles where predominantly same gender African-American men and women partied.

I went to "The Catch" like it was the thing to do. I was happy being around African-American men and women. At times, I wasn't very comfortable because I was still trying to stay in the closet.

Some nights, I didn't know who I would run into. I would try to play it safe. We would dance the night away until it was time to go home. Around that time, the club closed around 4:00 a.m.

The last song before the lights came on was Goapele's *Closer*. That's when all the grinding started and phone numbers would be exchanged. It was even possible to have sex on the dance floor because it was just that type of vibe.

I would meet guys and they would get my number. One night, I had too many drinks and miscommunicated my location for the night. The guy I was actually dating showed up and so did another guy I had a strong liking for. I couldn't think of anything to say to explain why I had two guys at the same place.

I always seemed to get into mixed-up triangle situations involving other people who liked me. I was continuing a pattern of lying while hiding in a world where I wanted to be comfortable, yet secretive.

I tried to keep them from realizing that I was trying to keep them apart. One was in the waiting area while one was on the dance floor. It all became too much. I ended up leaving the club without either one of them knowing.

When my phone started to ring, I knew what the questions would be, so I didn't answer until the next day. I made up another lie about why I left. In my eyes, it was better to deal with both of them over the phone than in person.

When I spotted people that I knew at the club, I would dance into the corner and look through a mirror where I could see them but they couldn't see me. If they were in the club, maybe they were doing the same thing I was doing.

It was tough trying to have a good time while looking for people I might know at the same time. Yet, for some reason it was fun. It was a thrill for me.

I knew I had it all together. I always said that I was going over to friend's houses whenever I was going to those clubs because I didn't want my mom to find out. I think she started to catch on when I began buying sexy underwear. I would like to believe that my mama knew, even when I was fighting it.

As much as I thought I was hiding something from her, she always knew. My mother never came out and asked me; she was waiting for me to tell her.

I wore sport underwear (as the box indicated), but they were almost close to thongs. I felt sexy in them. Depending on who I was dancing with, that person would get the chance to see them. How many drinks I had that night was also a factor.

I played that character for a while. He was my stripper persona. Something about "DRE" gave me confidence and sex appeal.

DRE knew what his intentions were before he left home. He knew exactly what underwear to put on. He knew to pack an overnight bag because he wasn't coming home after the club.

I remember my mom telling me not to come into her home at late hours of the night. Why did she do that? One night I lost track of time. When I looked up, it was way past the "curfew" she had set for me.

In my mind, I was a damn adult and I was being safe. I wasn't coming into her home all loud and wild with men I met at the club. I felt that I was being respectful.

I slept in my car in front of the house. I still didn't learn my lesson from that, so on other nights, I would stay with my dad. He never asked any questions.

DREW'S JOURNAL

May 10, 2004

Well, well, well... I don't know where to begin. Let's start off with the Kelly Price play, "Why Did I Get Married?" I liked the play, but I guess I liked the person I went with better.

After the play, we went to Santa Monica Blvd. Why did I fall in LOVE with Santa Monica? Now, we go every week and I get picked up by guys. That's fun to me.

I went last night after church and danced my ass off. I met this guy and we went to my car and did some things. Lord, have mercy! I don't even remember his name. Oh well, he didn't have my real name either.

I wanted to be discreet and safe. I thought I could get away with being in the clubs posing as someone who was just hanging with his friends. I needed to leave the scene for a while because I was blowing my own cover.

Over a period of time, people started talking. Word got out that I was a man on the DL (down low). Going to the clubs gave me the attention I wanted. It was good. It was what I thought I needed.

Growing up, I never went to clubs; especially same gender clubs. I always wanted to go but I couldn't get others to tag along.

It was easier being silent about my DL life because that was the Andrew that others didn't know. If they did know, they never said anything about it.

I was always cautious with the women I would sleep with. I never shared with any of them my other life because I was never going to confirm the rumors or confess to the "lifestyle."

Chapter 5

THIS IS

Y

I HID WHILE

I WAS IN

CHURCH

I considered being gay a curse. Being raised in the church instilled a strong religious background with Baptist roots. I kept my secrets buried.

I still wanted to be a part of church services. I enjoyed singing and teaching Bible studies. The more I remained silent about my homosexuality, the less people knew. People could assume all they wanted, but the truth would only be confirmed if I said something.

I didn't know who to be. I would go home at night and try to figure out why I had these feelings. Church was all I had grown accustomed to. My entire life was dedicated to the church. I didn't think that life existed outside of it.

I saw people making money while dedicating their lives to the church. I thought I could do the same, but I had to conceal who I was in order to do it.

If I missed a church service, I would feel bad because I felt like I was missing out on a "high time" of praise. Everyone in church knew "ANDREW." The older generation would say things to me like,

"The Holy Ghost is all in you, chile," or "Don't let the fire go out."

I loved church. It gave me a platform to perform. Church gave me a microphone and allowed me to sing! Church gave me a podium and allowed me to preach! Church also allowed me to wear a mask and hide in plain sight.

Chapter 6

THIS IS

Y

I ANSWERED
THE CALL

On Sunday, March 1, 1997, during an evening service at church, I went to the altar for prayer. Little did I know, my prayer would lead to a performance.

I didn't leave the altar when everyone else did. At the time, I thought I was wrestling with God about accepting the call to ministry. I remember that evening clearly. I never wanted to be a preacher! Everyone else wanted me to become a preacher. I saw how others accepted this "call" into the ministry, so I thought that was the way for me to go as well.

I remained at the altar for a long time and cried because that was the way to surrender to the call of God on your life. At the time of that performance, my youth pastor and his wife were by my side saying, "Say yes, Andrew! He wants a YES!"

I had to keep the struggle intense as if I was battling with angels. The "Yes" was hard to say because I was saying to myself "Oh, ok. Let me hurry up and get this over with!" I finally said "YES." More of the tears came and then I was weak. At the end, I was just standing there looking like an idiot.

I had secured yet another performance trophy. I said "Yes." I agreed to a "call" of pleasing others. I had to yield to other people's living arrangements they had made for me. It wasn't my life I was living anyway, right?

There were no clouds or smoke in the air. I didn't even see Jesus that night. I had no idea how he would look if I was supposed to see him.

No earthquake happened. No loud voice came from heaven to speak to me. No heavenly bells were ringing in my ear. I was caught up in the spiritual hype and emotion of it all.

I didn't feel any different than when I initially went to the altar. It was a performance. That's the only thing that comes to my mind.

It had no real meaning to me. It made other's prophecies come to pass while it confused me even more. *What did I get myself into? Why did I add this to my life? Was it not enough that I was already unhappy, that my life wasn't making sense? Now, I needed validation from the church?*

I always found myself lying! It was lie after lie after lie. I was covering up one lie to keep up with another lie and I believed them. I was making others believe a false persona of me.

How dare I go in front of the church and say I'm a homosexual? What prayer group could I actually go to that would say "Okay... and?" After all, it was the curse! It was evil. It was an abomination. Homosexuality is a sinful act. God loves the sinner, but hates the sin! It's a choice! It was a foul spirit and should be in hell! Instead, I chose to give the church something else to be proud of. I became a preacher.

I hated studying for sermons. I hated attending meetings that involved preparation for preachers. I didn't like the Bible College I was attending. I couldn't pay for it anyway, so I dropped out.

I didn't understand what the big hype was about being a preacher other than the fact that I was the only one speaking while others were listening. Lights, camera, action!

I started copying other preachers and their styles of preaching while taking their sermons and making them my own. I changed the sermon titles and made up my own. I would listen to tapes of other preachers and use their methods of delivery. I studied preaching like I would study for a character in a play.

I learned how to preach. I couldn't "hoop" like most preachers did to get the audience all riled up because I never really wanted to. I played the part. I was good at it and got away with it.

Church gave me a huge complex. Whenever I would hear a preacher speak about homosexuality, I always felt like he was targeting me. I would shout in agreement because I never knew who was watching to see if I was silent or appeared uncomfortable.

I would laugh at the homosexual jokes that really weren't funny. I would nod my head in disgust when homosexuality was preached. I would give my two cents on conversations with people who despised homosexuality. I wasn't ignorant, I just wasn't prepared for the comebacks.

I had no one to turn to or confide in. Everyone already talked too damn much about other homosexuals in the church. Everyone else's business was always juicier than the shit they kept in the closet or swept under the rug.

You couldn't be friends with people in the church without them placing labels on your friendship or suggesting a sexual relationship. It became too much. So, I suppressed it all those years by praying, praising, and fasting for divine deliverance to make me into a heterosexual.

I wanted to go out into the world and tell them that I had been changed. I had the script of deliverance in my head for that great day when I would say, "I have been delivered from homosexuality!" I heard people do it and it seemed so easy, but I was having a hard time with the transformation.

I had the entire testimony worked out in my head: "I once was gay, but now I'm a heterosexual. I was living a sinful, pathetic life. Although I lived my life as a homosexual, I knew that God didn't create me to be that way! I knew that I was intended to be with a woman, but I **chose** to be with men." *That* was going to be the powerful church shaking line.

I knew I was born gay. I didn't just pick it up one night and say, "Hey, I think I want to like boys!" I always knew I was different. I wasn't the average young man. I had different goals and aspirations in my life. I didn't want what others wanted.

My family encouraged me to play sports and I hated them. I still dislike them, but I played them because it was a popular thing to do. It kept them from harassing me.

Truthfully, I wanted to be a yell leader on the cheerleading squad. I never forgot the day I told some of my cousins and was laughed at. I was embarrassed because they said that's what girls did. I was already an outcast.

For the record, my father knew that I did not like sports, so he suggested acting to me. He saw that I had character.

I lived an entire lie in the church and for the church. The church and its followers rate homosexuality as one of its top 10 sins! I would often hear things like "If you sleep with people just don't be gay because the promises of God aren't entitled to gays." "Homosexuals can't go to heaven because it's an abomination unto God."

I choose not to use any scriptures from the Bible in this book to quote or use because we all know what they are and where they are. And if you don't, Google them or listen to the many preachers and pastors speak about it on YouTube.

I can understand how one chooses to kill themselves rather than deal with their reality because that was me. I chose to lie to myself for all those years because it was easier to do.

I deemed church to be my everything. If I was going to be anyone of note, it was going to be in the church! I held too many positions there and knew too many people in the church to let them down. I was a choir director, soloist, youth team leader, youth pastor, and a human. I built that fantasy in the church. It was a lie.

I became everything to everyone else for their approval and satisfaction. They would applaud me when I did something good and tell me, "You have a mighty work to do for the Lord." My audience in this performance were the people in my religion. If it pleased them, I was good.

My religion supported me as long as I was in the right relationship with them and their GOD. It didn't matter that I was struggling with finding my relation-ship with God because my relationship with my religion and the people associat-ed with it was more attainable anyway.

Church was my safe haven. Religion was the umbrella that kept me from get-ting wet. Church was all I thought there was. I thought like that because the church was all I knew.

Now, what? What happens after I say "yes" to my (calling)? You mean to tell me that I would be preaching about the Bible from the pulpit? That sacred and holy place? Oh, wow!

On July 12, 1998, I preached my very first sermon from the pulpit at Christ Second Baptist Church. The church was full that evening. The title of my message was "Midnight Mission" coming from Acts 16:25. "And at midnight Paul and Silas prayed and sang praises unto GOD." I got that verse from listening to Fred Hammonds Live CD.

It sounded soul stirring. I attempted in my own way to mimic the exhorter's approach. The title came from a mission in Downtown Los Angeles that I saw when driving a few days before my debut. I knew it was a sign from God that it had to be my sermon's title.

That night, it was showtime. I wore a shiny silver suit and had a yellow paper tablet with the notes I had written down. My nerves were all over the place because I had to make sure I preached just right.

I didn't know what the hell I was doing. There were a lot of people in there listening and paying close attention to every word I spoke. Action!

The first sermon is always the one that will make or break you. I was thankful that the folks had a high time rejoicing before I walked to the podium because my sermon sucked! It went down like the *Titanic*. At least to me, it was horrible. I was all over the place and it was a lot harder than I ever thought.

After the service I asked myself, "Why did you get up there and do that?" Since so many of my friends were accepting their call into the ministry, I felt it was my time, too.

I stayed up late writing sermons that I thought would make the crowd go wild and get some type of reaction out of them. I also had to be sure to make three points and share the gospel of Jesus Christ. You couldn't say you preached the gospel until you hung Christ on the cross, buried Him, and in three days brought Him back to life.

Everything had to tie into the sermon. "Christ was born to the Virgin Mary. He had no home (organ cues up). Christ had no home. He went to Calvary. They beat Him, mocked Him, and pierced Him in the side, but in three days... I said, BUT in three days, He got up with allllllll power in his hands! He gave us power to heal the sick! He gave us power to raise the dead! He left us with that Holy Ghost power!"

People would get excited about the cross. People would yell, "Yes, **preach**!" I could've been preaching about molasses and ants, but it all had to conclude at the cross.

Preaching was added pressure for me. It might have come easily to others, but to me, it wasn't right. I still did it.

I was giving up my Saturday evenings to study for the message on Sunday. If I couldn't make up a sermon, I would find one. I would listen to tapes and change it up a bit.

In spite of all that, I enjoyed being a Youth Pastor the most. I believe it was because I was one of them. I was more like a leader. I was their friend. I loved each and every one of them from a special place in my heart. I connected with all of them in ways they didn't know.

I wanted so many times to share with them what I was dealing with, but I feared that they would go home and tell their parents. Then, the parents would have taken their youth out of my Bible study class. I didn't want anyone thinking that I was trying to change them or their theology. To them, I just wanted to be Andrew or Drew. Then came "Pastah Drew."

At times, I wanted to leave the youth ministry because I was always talking about being true and loving yourself. The whole time, I was lying and not loving myself. I would wipe their tears, yet hide my own. They trusted me and I trusted most of them.

No, I never thought of doing sexual things with them and no, I never had any crushes on any of my youth—male or female. That wasn't in me. I wasn't ever trying to teach or preach anything in reference to homosexuality. It was a topic that I was uncomfortable discussing with my youth ministry.

There was a time when I presented lessons about homosexuality because I wanted to get the youth's view on it. I wanted to see how much understanding they had. So, I had them teach it. Some of the things I heard and read would make anyone continue living life behind a mask.

I was afraid. What would they think if I ever told them about me? So, for the sake of the church's reputation and the respect I already had from my youth, I remained silent.

I kept my thoughts to myself. I would bring women around to make everyone think I was looking for love. I wanted whatever they heard or may have thought to be thrown off.

Women were my cover. People would get a glimpse of different women who would show up for me at the church. I would have women on both sides of the audience during church services. Some nights, I would have a man. I had to keep both worlds from colliding. I couldn't have them finding out about each other.

Chapter 7

THIS IS

Y

I LIED TO

THE WOMEN

IN MY LIFE

While I was in the clubs and having sex with men, I was still dating women to validate my manhood. I always knew that I was gay. I had always known about my sexuality from my early years in life.

I never did the normal things guys would do. I always hung around girls. When I had birthday parties, girls would show up. I couldn't share my true feelings because I never wanted to be harassed.

I had girlfriends throughout every level of school. I wasn't unattractive. I went through my ugly phase, but it didn't stop me from getting the girls. My first kiss was behind the kickball diamond at Bixby Elementary School.

I was different to the point of always standing out. My voice never matched me. Most guys thought I was a "sissy" because my voice was so soft and I had a lisp that I was very ashamed of.

I hated going to school. I was always being talked about. After hearing them gossip, I found myself shutting down and became very uncomfortable being me. So, I found another life to portray.

I dated in high school and actually fell in love a couple of times. In order to try to fit in, I began to put on false airs to convince others that I had it "going on."

My girlfriend at the time had a car. Whenever she would drop me off, I would have her take me over to my grandmother's house down the street from where I actually lived. One day, she called me because she wanted to drop off a card. My grandmother wasn't home, so I had to break the truth to her about where I really lived. I was embarrassed about my place of residence. Why? Our family of five lived in a two-bedroom apartment. I felt like I had to lie to be something or someone I wasn't. So, I grew up lying.

After my divorce, I decided I wasn't going to date anymore. Getting over my marriage was my excuse for not dating. If anyone would ask why I had not returned to the world of dating, that would be my response. "Well… you know… I'm just getting out of a divorce…" Instead of just dating them, I made them my friends.

Some would be my lady friends with benefits. I would never attach myself to them but they would attach themselves to me. I would sleep with them to prove that I was a man and to feed my ego.

I knew that I was good in bed. I thought that if I gave them a good time, it would be enough. I was only pleasing my inconsiderate, whorish ego.

My lady friends were beautiful, wholesome, intelligent, and classy. Some went to church, while others didn't. When a woman would tell me that she was saving herself for marriage, she immediately became my prey. I was a predator. I had to make it known to her and me that I was going to get her.

It didn't matter that she went to church. It didn't matter if she had just rededicated her life back to God. All of that was more reason for me to go after her. Some just took a little longer.

Whatever I didn't have, they made sure I had it. I cared for all of them, but never committed myself to them. I would make them believe they were the only one.

I had no intention of ever being with any of them. Some would call it trickery. Some would call it deceit. Some would say it was all manipulation. The reality is, it was a lie. I now understand how homosexuality can be viewed by so many with such hatred because some homosexuals lie to others while lying to themselves.

I was playing yet another character. I had a new script to follow. I was so consumed with my performances that I failed to recognize the sincerity in those women.

It was difficult to appreciate and recognize people who wanted nothing from me but me. Unfortunately, I could not give a woman me because I didn't know who I was. I just knew the basics. I was a man who was gay, professing to be someone other than who I was.

Why am I revealing all of this now? I was too much of a coward back then to acknowledge it.

DREW'S JOURNAL

June 26, 2003

I'm closing chapters in my life, whether complete or incomplete, good or bad. I still need a lot of work on my mouth and my desires of sleeping with women for the stroking of my ego.

I know I have no business talking to her the way I have, knowing damn well that I'm not the least bit interested in her. "Lisa," on the other hand, is a different story. If she feels that buying me meals is all I get, then what is going to happen when I start losing weight?

As bad as I hate to close the chapter with "Sally," it has now come to an end. I can't stand knowing that she has a guy in her life. Oh, well. That's life.

On a brighter note, my soon to be ex-wife just called. It shocked the hell out of me. Her voice made me feel some type of way. I fell for her all over again just because she called.

Nooooo! She's supposed to hate me. I'm crazy. I'm tripping out that she called. I want to see her. I want to kiss her right now. Let me pull myself together because I'm not in the right mind frame to go back into that.

DREW'S JOURNAL

March 2, 2004

What have I gotten myself into? Where am I headed? I know damn well I didn't just commit myself to this man. Oh, my God.

This is so bad and I know it is. I know I am out of the will of God. I can't even fake the funk. He is a real nice-looking guy and he is actually digging me.

If anyone found out this side of me, they wouldn't know what to say. How much longer can I actually hold this in? Who am I fooling? Why am I doing this? My life makes no sense to me right now.

My last day on my job was Friday. I'm unemployed at the moment. When I read this in the future, I'll see the crap I put myself into.

DREW'S JOURNAL

March 18, 2004

Oh, well... I told someone. I told her my secret. I found myself telling her all of the secrets that had to do with my other life.

I felt comfortable being honest with her for some reason. There was no judgment. She just listened to me and nodded.

I was laying on her floor, spilling out my life to her. She has known me from a child and here I was releasing a part of myself to her. I was trying to spin her into my web of women, but she had a plan of her own to get me to confess. It wasn't forced; she did it with calmness. It was almost too easy.

She already had her thoughts about me. If she already thinks this about me, I wonder who else was thinking like this?

I'm tired of living this lie. I want God to use me in every way fit so that He will get the glory. God, why do I have to be this way? This just didn't come upon me.

As a child, I was playing with Barbie dolls. I even went into the same bathroom stall with a guy in elementary. I liked wrestlers and their bodies.

I began experimenting with guys at a young age. I just need to deal with these issues and face them with my Heavenly Father. I should take it to God and be like, "Here it is... all of it!"

If a woman is going to be with me, she needs to know all of my mess. I don't want her in the dark about anything concerning me. I want her to know she has a man that has had some real-life issues. It's all good. I thank God for placing her in my life.

My mom told me today that she was ashamed of me for smoking weed. That really hurt, but I still want to smoke the rest of this joint.

I told myself that I don't want to work for anybody. I just want to do drama and get paid for it. I know the Lord will supply, but my life has to be right. I don't want to be a perpetrating pastor. I need to get some type of spirituality back into my life.

As you can tell from my previous journal entries, I was all over the place with no direction. I was struggling with who I was. I had made up my mind that being gay was a curse. My curse. My thorn to bear. It was a conflict of my origin.

I wanted to like women, but I just couldn't keep my attention on just one. I didn't know who to be. I would go home and wrestle with God and become upset because a change wasn't happening, no matter how many times I fasted.

I thought that masturbation was my struggle, so if I masturbated while thinking about women, maybe that would change me. It didn't. In order for me to sleep with women, I would often drink liquor so that it would have a mind of its own. I had to drink to keep myself at attention. I merely wanted it all to make sense to me. Why did I have these feelings for men?

I began to search for a way to reach an understanding. Myths of homosexuality say that if a father isn't present in the home, men tend to seek that presence in other men. That was wrong. My father was in the home at all times and I didn't grow up without one.

Another one says that if a young man was raped or molested at a young age, the trauma would convince him to believe that he was gay. Again, all wrong. I wasn't raped or molested by anyone. No family member touched me or made me do anything sexual. I wasn't forced to have sex with anyone. The people I surrounded myself with respected my family.

"Well, it's a choice…" Wow! Really? A choice? Who chooses to be heterosexual? Who chooses to be homosexual? Does a dog pick and choose what kind of dog he wants to be? Who chooses to be a male? Who chooses to be a female from birth?

We can choose our pets. We can choose our homes. We can choose our careers. We can choose our friends. I believe that we don't and can't choose our own nationality or sexuality.

My sexuality is a wonderful gift from my Creator. Our God. Everything about me was all a part of the divine plan.

Yes, I was born this way and I accept it. Five fingers, five toes, one nose, two ears, one mouth, two eyes and (points down) **that**! There is nothing about me that was a mistake.

I chose to identify with who people wanted me to be. That was my mistake. I wasn't sure I could handle the pressure from others. I was genetically induced with chromosomes to make me a homosexual. I am a gift of life.

I wrestled with the Scriptures. I read them and saw the word "homosexuality" and knew I wasn't going to be accepted into heaven. Instead, I choose to make my heaven here on earth but I only ended up creating a hell for myself.

I wanted to understand me why a loving God would hate me. I would hear people say, "God doesn't hate the homosexual, he hates the **sin**." I'm not a sin!

How was I created in His image but not invited to dwell in the afterlife with Him? How could He say I was good, but wasn't entitled to the promises of God? How could He be my Father while I was being treated like an outcast? It made no sense.

I was hiding for others to like me. I hid because I was afraid. Then they said I'm not a sin, but the lifestyle I chose is. What? That is like picking and choosing who our parents are. I couldn't take it anymore. I got tired of defending who I was.

Chapter 8

THIS IS

Y

I WANTED

TO COMMIT

SUICIDE

I was sitting at work when I felt a war raging inside of me. I was an emotional wreck and blanked out. I had to leave. I called my mom and I told her what was going on in my head. She prayed for me but that didn't stop my thoughts or what I was planning.

I didn't tell anyone what I was thinking because I didn't want anyone to stop me. I took the rest of the day off and went home. Tears were in my eyes the entire way. I didn't want to hurt myself or cause any bodily harm. I just wanted to sleep and not wake up again.

I wasn't going to leave a note. I had no intention of informing anyone. I was going to take all of my prescription pills and just wait to doze off. I had Vicodin, Norco, and Oxytocin in front of me. I was staring at the bottles and crying because I wasn't afraid anymore. I knew what I had to do to escape. If I woke up, my plan failed. I was determined not to wake up again.

Intervention happened because I was in such a hurry to die that I didn't lock my front door. My friend showed up. I didn't say anything to her. She saw the pills, looked at me and said, "What are you doing?" With tears still in my eyes, I couldn't respond. I just cried.

I wanted to tell her why but I couldn't bring myself to tell her. She was a great friend and had romantic feelings for me. Why did she have to show up and make me deal with my reality of masking up yet again?

I wasn't ready to tell her the real truth behind my actions because I knew she wasn't ready. I wasn't in a place to deal with her pain. She was a great friend and I had pursued her.

Suicide should never be an option for anyone but when it feels like you are alone, it can seem like the only choice. It's always easier for someone to advise you not to give up. They aren't dealing with the internal voices inside of you, so it feels like they can't relate.

The voices became so loud inside my head that I just wanted to silence them. I had to make it to a place where I said enough is enough.

It was then that I decided to create my play entitled "Y." It is a series of monologues, spoken word, and dance segments interpreting the stories of my life. Each character was a part of me at some point and represented me in some way.

I wrote my story as a way to heal. I didn't know it at the time, but I see where I was in the beginning stages of telling my story. I just kept writing until I tapped into the uncomfortable places in my life and exposed myself. Still, I wasn't telling anyone what I was doing but I knew it had to be done.

One of my favorite characters was J.R. He was the homosexual son of a church going family. In the play, he read the letter that he wrote before he committed suicide. He wrote everything he wanted to tell his family as his final goodbye. Writing that part of the play was difficult because I knew I was beginning to reveal my own story.

I was preparing myself based on the responses of a character. Once again, I found myself working to make sure that others were okay with a story they were seeing on stage. I didn't know the impact the play would have, but by the emails and messages I got, I knew the message was well-received. It made me glad.

I pressed into an area that finally opened the doors for conversations to flow. I realized I had to move forward. I couldn't keep promoting a message of truth and forgiveness while lying. The message impacted me to the point that I had reached a place with my truth.

Suicide wanted to take the human that I was out. I was going to commit myself to death, but what I didn't realize was that I was already the walking dead. For so many years, I was dead to Andrew but trying to live a version of alternate reality. Out of the suicide attempt came a life I can live to now write about.

THE MASK

Brother, which one will you put on today? I hope it's not me because the last time you put me on, you still didn't smile. You were still crying deep down inside.

Let me talk to you for a minute, if I may. Why do you hide your face behind me every day? I cover up your past, your failures, and all of your mistakes just so you can perpetrate to everyone that you aren't a fake. Deep down, you're afraid for people to see you before you put me on so they can applaud a performance well done.

You've used me too often because of all the hurt you've been through. You won't speak up for anything because you're afraid of what people may say about you. When you look in the mirror, what or who do you really see? A perfect mask and a fake wannabe.

You wanna be rich, you wanna be fine, you wanna be with those who validate you from time to time. Wake up and see the beauty that God resides in you.

Honestly, you really don't need me. Give me a rest. Put me away. Save me for kids to wear on Halloween or for a stage play.

You shouldn't have to hide who you really are and the issues you wrestle with inside. You shouldn't have to plead for someone to accept your insanity. Show who you really are and unveil the mask for the world to see.

You are a mess, but a good work in progress. It's okay go ahead and cry for the pain you hid behind so long. Today, it's got to die. Who cares what they have to say?

You are unique; that's why you have your own birthday. You hid behind me for so long that you started to believe I could take your pain away. Every time you took me off, you were still left with the shame and guilt to face the next day.

It's okay that you were hurt, I know your pain. You don't have to go on living your life behind a masquerade. I hope you're not mad at me, but I had to let you know that whatever you are hiding, it's time to let it go. Let them see you—even the mistakes that you will make. If you were perfect, you would be like me—a face people put on in times of misery.

Chapter 9

THIS IS

Y

This is my truth now and current state of living. If I could do things differently that wouldn't have affected so many wonderful people in my life, I would. I'm a better person now.

I apologize to every female I misled and lied to. I apologize for the tears you cried because of my lies. I apologize to the girlfriends I dated and used as cover-ups for people to believe that I was a heterosexual man. I apologize to my ex-wife for taking her down an altar in hopes that marriage would change my way of living.

You have all been wonderful people in my life and I thank you for the lasting friendships we still have. I was extremely selfish and wanted the best of both worlds, no matter the repercussions.

An apology may never be enough for the tears you cried or the hurt I caused. I betrayed your trust. For that, I apologize. I always thought of your feelings and your genuine hearts. It always crossed my mind how it would affect you when you actually knew my truth.

I apologize to the many church members I hurt because my lies. What I did on Sunday mornings was an expression of my love for God. If I had been honest, I don't believe you would have allowed me to stand in a pulpit, lead worship services, or even teach your youth.

My love for the youth has always been a purpose in my life. I never wanted anything less than the best for them. No, I never wanted to molest any of them. I didn't have any secret agendas with the young men. I never desired any of them in an inappropriate manner.

I loved my experience being a Youth Pastor and inspiring young people. Many of them helped my days in church to be a lot more bearable. I wanted to display strength. At other times, I wanted to run and hide when I heard things about myself that hurt. I knew about the emails, telephone conversations, and mindless chatter about me, but I didn't have the strength to fight back or retaliate. It was the truth, but I couldn't admit it.

To my youth reading this book right now, I apologize for teaching you to be honest when I was lying. Each of you has impacted my life in a special way. I would not trade any of our time together. I just wish I could've told you all personally so you wouldn't have to hear it from other sources. I need to apologize because I may never hear from you, but I want you to know my heart.

I wrote this book for myself first. I wanted to tell on myself and help someone else get through their experiences. I know I'm not the only one with a story to share. My purpose in life is to serve and I want my life and words to live on forever.

My life has taken on a tremendous change since I came into myself. I don't profess to know everything, but I can say that I am constantly evolving and loving every minute of it. I may not express my love for God the way everyone else does, but I do have a sincere love for my Creator.

As far as the call on my life goes, I have answered it. It's not to pastor a congregation. It has nothing to do with church. I just want to live a life free of lies and deception.

Now, I'm at a place where I can say I am free. I am free to be me. I am free to live. I am free to express my sexuality. The sexuality I hid for so many years is being expressed daily while I have breath. Although my name is still the same, the person you once knew is no longer there.

Made in the USA
Columbia, SC
27 August 2020